Globalising HR

The Chartered Institute of Personnel and Development is the leading publisher of books and reports for personnel and training professionals, students, and all those concerned with the effective management and development of people at work. For full details of all our titles, please contact the Publishing Department:

Tel: 020 8263 3387
Fax: 020 8263 3850

E-mail: publish@cipd.co.uk

View the full range of CIPD titles on the CIPD website:
www.cipdpublishing.co.uk

Globalising HR

Chris Brewster

Hilary Harris

Paul Sparrow

First published 2002
Reprinted 2004

Cover design by Curve
Designed and typeset by Beacon GDT
Printed in Great Britain by Short Run Press

British Library Cataloguing in Publication Data
A catalogue record for this book is available from the British Library

ISBN 0 85292 971 4

Chartered Institute of Personnel and Development,
CIPD House, Camp Road, London SW19 4UX

Tel: 020 8971 9000
Fax: 020 8263 3333
Website: www.cipd.co.uk

Incorporated by Royal Charter. Registered charity no. 1079797.

Contents

Acknowledgements

The CIPD would like to thank the authors of the Executive Briefing, Professor Chris Brewster, Dr Hilary Harris and Professor Paul Sparrow and their colleagues for the research and preparation necessary.

Thanks also go to current CIPD Vice President International, John Campbell, and former Vice Presidents Bob Morton and Peter Squire and their International Panel and Forum for supporting and contributing to the research.

The CIPD is deeply appreciative of members of the Institute and the companies and individuals who took the time to complete survey questionnaires and be interviewed for case studies, which has made this research possible.

Fran Wilson

CIPD, International Manager

Foreword

This Executive Briefing reports the outcomes of the flagship project on global HRM that started in late 2000 and was completed in March 2002. Not only was it one of the first such research projects of its kind but it is the first time any comparable organisation anywhere in the world has devoted significant resources to this area.

The idea of a flagship project on global HRM appropriately came out of a discussion at an International HRM conference in the USA that I was attending in 1999 as Vice President International of the CIPD. At the conference there were many disparate ideas and contributions on the topic of International People Management, but no cohesive view or even an overview of the challenges facing HR professionals in what was an increasingly important field of HR practice, given that the internationalisation of business economies and management was one of the most striking features of employment in the closing years of the twentieth century.

In discussion with Professor Chris Brewster, both Frances Wilson of the CIPD and I felt that the CIPD could not only add to the body of knowledge and practice in the International HR field but that from the Institute's unique practitioner base we could contribute some leading-edge insight into practical international HRM. I am pleased to say that Ward Griffiths, who at the time was responsible for Professional Knowledge and Information in the Institute, strongly supported the idea of a major research project, which has now come to fruition.

The CIPD is keen to raise awareness among its membership that globalisation is relevant and important to all members, as they are increasingly likely to have to function with regard to an international context, even when their organisation may not transact its primary business beyond a domestic front. As a signal of the increasing importance of the topic, International Personnel and Development was included as a component of the new CIPD Standards for Professional Qualification scheme launched in 2002. The present research by the CIPD now underpins a raised awareness of the importance of internationalisation in the work of members of the human resource management profession in the UK.

The purpose of this study was to draw together the disparate threads of what is known practically and academically in order to achieve the dual objectives of providing a broad, coherent overview of the field of international HRM along with a detailed, practical analysis of what is needed to be successful in this crucial area of modern management. To do this we were looking for answers to the following sorts of question:

- What models of organisation are being used to identify best practice in IHRM to support the business?
- What are an organisation's options in terms of its overall approaches to internationalisation?
- What do those options mean in terms of the way the organisation delivers global HRM?
- What skills will effective HRM practitioners need?

The research was undertaken by three of our leading academics in the International HRM field, Professor Chris Brewster, Dr Hilary Harris and Professor Paul Sparrow, and has involved experienced IHRM practitioners drawing on a strong practical case-studies basis as a foundation. I think the study has met its aims, and this Executive Briefing outlines its main findings, which will be reported in more depth in future publications.

Bob Morton

Chair, CIPD International Forum

Methodology

The CIPD project used three linked methodologies: two surveys and a repeating series of case studies.

The first survey was a web-based questionnaire designed to get the views of HR practitioners about IHRM. It was run in early 2001, and 732 respondents – CIPD members from the UK and Ireland – replied. In total their organisations employed 2.4 million staff. The average organisation size was 2,800 employees, with 400 employees in the UK.

The second survey was designed to examine the policies of international organisations in the UK, and 65 organisations took part in the study: 70 per cent of them employed more than 5,000 employees, 50 per cent had operations in more than 10 countries, 41 per cent had revenues above £100 million and there was a broad sectoral spread.

The report also draws upon insights from seven case studies developed over a year. These case studies involved 62 interviews with HR directors, business managers and service providers, attendance at key HR strategy workshops within the organisations, and use of internal documentation and external press search. Fieldwork was conducted in the UK, France, Belgium, the Netherlands and Singapore. In addition managers who had geographical responsibility for the USA, Australia, Germany, Ireland, Brazil, Vietnam, Ghana, Kenya, South Asia, East Asia, North Asia and Japan were interviewed. The interviews examined: the strategic nature of the HR interventions; the political, process and technical skills brought to bear; the contrasting stakeholder expectations of the interventions, role; and the link to organisational strategy and effectiveness.

Seven organisations took part in the case studies:

- Shell People Services (SPS) – focusing on the web-based provision of global HR services and knowledge transfer across four global businesses through the development of communities of practice

- Rolls-Royce plc – focusing on the experiences of a UK-centric company going global and the pursuit of a global centre of excellence strategy, and development of new areas of business through international joint venture working

- Diageo – focusing on convergence around core performance capability management, rewards and talent development processes and decentralisation of global HR through the use of global networks

- Stepstone.com – focusing on the internationalisation of HR in an e-commerce setting and the management of a start-up venture under intense competition

- BOC Group – focusing on the alignment of Asian HR country management with global lines of business that had been established in all other regional geographies

- ActionAid – focusing on international management in a not-for-profit but very international organisation

- Pacific Direct – focusing on internationalisation processes in an SME context.

Executive summary

- The effect of international operations and activities on HRM is enormous; and the impact of effective global HRM can make a major contribution to the success of an organisation's international operations.

- There is a critical difference between international HRM (which focuses on managing an internationally mobile workforce) and global HRM (which is concerned with managing international HRM activities through the application of global rule-sets).

The key drivers for international operations are:

- Maximising shareholder value
- Forging strategic partnerships
- Creating core business processes
- Building global presence

Of course, any one organisation may well exhibit several of these drivers at the same time.

The key delivery mechanisms for HRM are:

- E-enabling HR
- Knowledge management
- Cost reduction/HR affordability
- Creating centres of excellence

Again, any one organisation may have to work on several of these issues at once.

Global HRM activities tend to fall into one of three main areas:

- Transactional
- Capability development
- Business development

There is no one best way to manage global HRM. When the organisational drivers for internationalisation are well understood, when the key delivery mechanisms are in place, coherent and consistent, and when these mesh with the global HRM activities, then global HRM can make a significant contribution to organisational success. Where any one of these factors is absent, there will be problems.

Four key drivers of global HR are examined:

- **Maximising shareholder value**
- **Forging strategic partnerships**
- **Creating core business processes**
- **Building global presence**

along with four key enablers:

- **Rationalisation of costs**
- **Knowledge management**
- **E-enablement of HRM**
- **Centres of excellence on a global scale**

1 | Drivers and enablers of global HR

Our research programme uncovered four key drivers in the internationalisation of organisations. Interestingly, many of the other suggestions that have been put forward (sector competition or diminishing home markets, for example) did not feature as key drivers. The key drivers were:

- **Maximising shareholder value**
  In some cases maximising shareholder value was an implicit business objective. In others it was more plainly stated. Thus, when it was established, Diageo made clear commitments to its shareholders on the new conglomerate's performance within a stated time period. Internet job market provider Stepstone was having problems surviving in a highly competitive field and needed to keep its shareholders with it.

- **Forging strategic partnerships**
  The not-for-profit charity Action Aid had as a central part of its strategy the importance of decentralising activities to local operations and local staff. This involved working closely with other aid groups to ensure delivery of the necessary support. Rolls-Royce plc was keen to develop its partnerships with airlines, aircraft builders and suppliers – which meant being where they were.

- **Creating core business processes**
  Global HRM responds to the development of core business processes and the movement away from country-based operations towards business-line driven organisations. However, it does more than just respond. It is often a key part of the reorientation of strategy. Thus, for example, as Shell changed its business from oil extraction to retailing and refocused on centres of excellence around the world, HR had to arrange the staffing, procedures and policies to put that change in place and embed it within the organisation. BOC set up a Pacific-based operation and HR had to ensure that it worked.

- **Building global presence**
  Rolls-Royce identified an increasingly global market for aero engines, with much of the business in North America; it was important for them to have a presence there. As an internet-based company, Stepstone was inevitably international, but needed to make its operations match its reach. Pacific Direct had operations in China, the Czech Republic and the USA almost as soon as its total number of employees reached double figures; again, it needed to be visible where its markets were.

Figure 1 | Business drivers

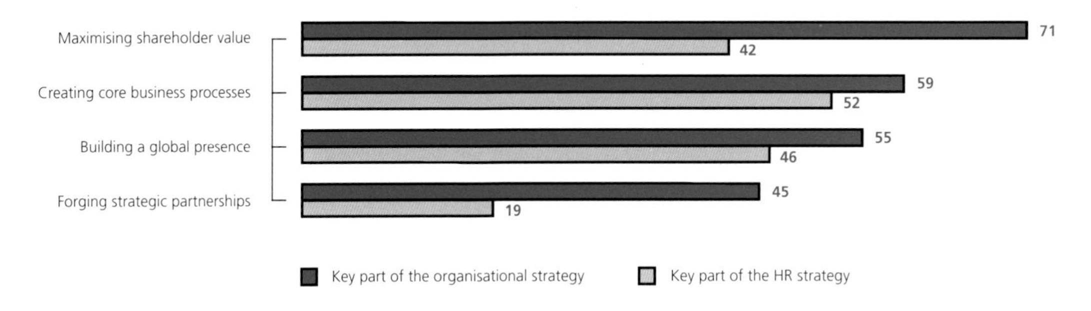

Figure 2 | Key delivery mechanisms

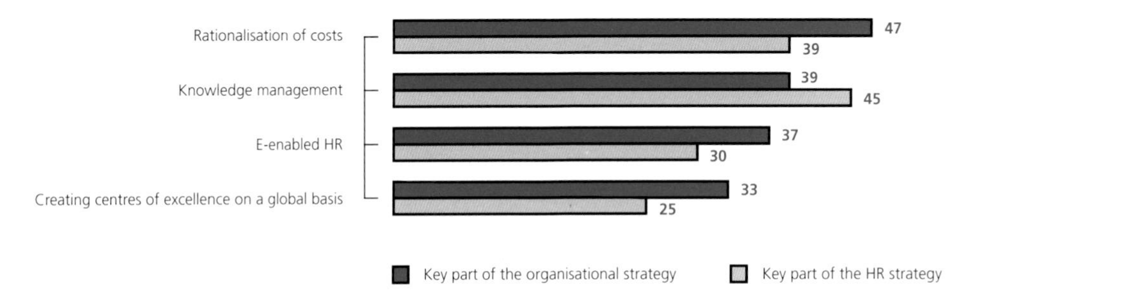

Our study found that the HR function used four key delivery mechanisms to respond to these drivers. These are:

- **Rationalisation of costs**
  Organisations are devoting much attention to ensuring they are putting their people where they can be most cost-effective and that central overheads are as low as possible. Behind most global HR functions' recent restructuring efforts has been the need to deliver global business strategies in the most cost-efficient manner possible. This is not to be confused with 'cheapest possible' – although it sometimes feels that way – because many of the companies we saw are making substantial investments in getting things right. But they are assessing their activities to cut out duplication and waste, to ensure added value and to move from purely *transactional* work, which can often be delivered directly by new technology, towards those activities that deal with *capability* and *business development*. There is an increased interest in an organisation's ability to measure the output of the HR function, reflecting the need to be able to deliver cost reductions and ensure HR affordability.

Knowledge management

Linked to the capability function is an increased focus on knowledge management. So far, largely perhaps because much of this debate has been driven by technical specialists, the possibilities of global HRM as the process that adds to and helps exploit the knowledge stock, and particularly the powerful intrinsic knowledge stock, have not been fully explored. But changes are happening that are putting pressure on company intranets and on the technology. But the HR function also has to grapple with the intrinsic knowledge held in people's heads that is often the key to competitive advantage. Hence global HR departments are taking on responsibility for the conscious development of operating networks, both as practitioners within the HR community and as facilitators elsewhere in the organisation.

E-enablement of HRM

Part of the response to these joint pressures is the pursuit of better ways to do things. A key challenge facing HRM is new information and communication technology. This applies across the board, but the impact on global HRM could be immense. Many of those companies we spoke to had started down this path: none felt they were anywhere other than at the beginning of it; but most realised that it would dramatically change what HRM could do. The ability to get HRM information to and from, and support on to, line managers' desks without a formal HRM intervention opens up new and exciting possibilities, which may allow HR to focus on its capability and business development roles. The e-enablement of HR is being engineered on a global basis. Organisations such as Diageo and Rolls-Royce find that they have different systems and software packages in many business functions – HR included. Over time these systems will have to be integrated, often within the guise of centralised business services. Organisations such as Ford and Shell have global e-enablement programmes, with their HR Online and Galaxy initiatives respectively.

Centres of excellence on a global scale

One way of achieving some of the previous objectives, and one with intrinsic value, is the creation of centres of excellence. Rolls-Royce, for example, neither wants all work to be carried out in its UK headquarters nor to replicate such capabilities everywhere it operates. Centres of excellence spread across the globe are the obvious way forward, and part of the response, in HR as elsewhere, is the move towards developing such centres. In many instances, the HR function itself is also being viewed as a series of centres of excellence best organised on a global basis. Sometimes these are carefully calculated decisions: the organisation makes informed and rational changes to its HR structure, based on decisions about where its true competence in specific HR processes really resides around the world. More often, it appears that the decisions are based on small groups of specialists with an interest; and sometimes even individuals with a real commitment to an issue have made it their own and start to gather others around them, often through virtual networks.

'The HR function also has to grapple with the intrinsic knowledge held in people's heads that is often the key to competitive advantage.'

This chapter finds that:

- **Global HRM has a much more strategic role than domestic HRM, including input into the critical 'global versus local' debate**
- **Many global organisations do not need to pass through the classic 'stages of internationalisation'**
- **No organisation in the survey thought it had yet achieved a fully geocentric orientation**
- **There are 10 main challenges facing global HR functions**

2 | Is there a difference between global and domestic HRM?

Ask any self-respecting HR professional what the critical determinant of success for their function is and you will almost certainly get the response: 'Being a strategic partner for the business.' Some of the processes and capabilities for achieving this are well known to all of us working in HR: the need for board-level representation, the ability to fully understand the business, the need for excellent analytical and planning skills, the ability to measure the effectiveness of HR interventions, etc. The present study clearly demonstrates that being a strategic partner for the business is not the same thing for HR professionals working in domestically based organisations as for their colleagues working in international organisations. Our research reveals, generally, a much more strategic role for the global HR function, with additional knowledge and abilities required on the part of HR professionals.

A critical aspect of creating effective global HR strategies is the ability to judge the extent to which an organisation should implement similar practices across the world or adapt them to suit local conditions – the 'global versus local' debate. This key challenge requires a high level of strategic thinking on the part of global HR professionals. While scanning the world for best practice, they need to ensure that the policies and practices they implement are appropriate to the unique nature of their international operations. Clearly, there is no 'one best way' of how to run a strategic global HR function. The nature of the strategic role played by HR in international organisations depends on their degree of internationalisation, rather than other factors such as sector or industry categorisation. So how do we assess how international an organisation is? Possible approaches could include:

- geographical spread
- degree of 'transnationality':
  - ratio of foreign assets to total assets
  - foreign sales to total sales
  - foreign employment to total employment
- production of 'global' products
- global integration of processes.

While these categories might be useful from an economic perspective, they do not help identify the most effective way of managing structure and people in international organisations. Most of us are aware of the 'stages of internationalisation' approach, which suggests that organisations will need to follow very different HRM policies and practices according to the relevant stage of international corporate evolution. However, the world of business is changing, with many start-up businesses global from the outset. Our study casts doubt on the assumption that organisations will progress through each stage. Stepstone and Pacific Direct are examples of new international start-ups that attempt (and need) to move straight to the global stage in order to capture the advantages of rapidly globalising markets. For example, Stepstone had to move within a one-year period from employing 200 people in five countries to employing 1,400 people in 18 countries. At the same time, rapidly changing business fortunes meant that its global HR function had to deal with *plan sociale* in its French operations and the creation of outsourced data processing operations from the UK to India, among many other challenges.

Even in mature businesses there might be a need to establish rapidly an international presence in a new business area through the use of joint ventures. Rolls-Royce had to manage similarly rapid internationalisation in its engine repair and overhaul business, moving from five primarily UK operations to 17 worldwide operations in under five years.

While the 'stage' approach is an over-simplification, it demonstrates that there is a link between *how* an international organisation structures itself and the *philosophy* that it holds about managing its human resources. This can range from a situation where all the power rests with headquarters to a truly global orientation where the organisation takes a worldwide approach to its operations, recognising that each part makes a unique contribution with its own special competence.

Our results showed that most, but not all, organisations in our survey and in the case studies are aiming towards a global orientation in which top management is striving to create an integrated organisation (see Figure 3). Two-thirds of our survey respondents agreed with the statement 'Top management strives to create an integrated organisation' as a description of their organisation's management strategy. However, this may not mean that they are practising a fully geocentric strategy. The case studies showed that there are no organisations that believe they have got there yet.

Two key conclusions can be drawn from this analysis of the role of the HR function in international organisations:

- The added value of the HR function in an international organisation lies in its ability to manage the delicate balance between overall co-ordinated systems and sensitivity to local needs, including cultural differences, in a way that aligns with both business needs and senior management philosophy.

- There is a distinction between international HRM and global HRM. Traditionally, international HRM has been about managing an international workforce – the expatriates, frequent commuters, cross-cultural team members and specialists involved in international knowledge transfer. Global HRM is not simply about covering these staff around the world. It concerns managing international HRM activities through the application of global rule-sets.

The main challenges faced by global HR functions are very varied, but can be considered under ten generic headings (see Box 1 on page 10).

Figure 3 | Management strategy

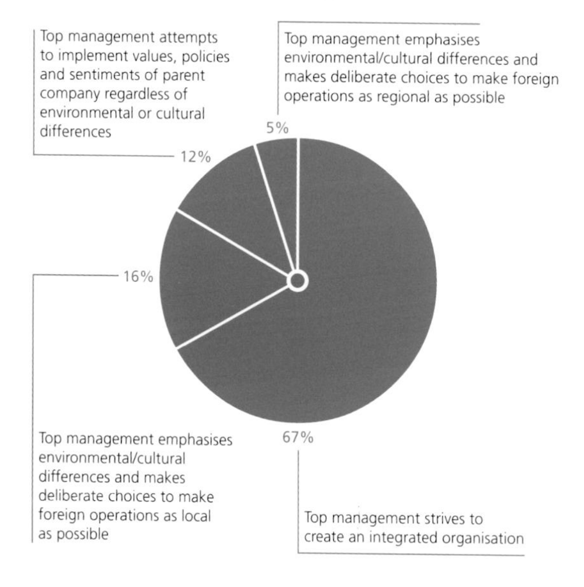

'...Today, most people believe that there is a set of global processes. However, in [this company], when people use the word "global" they mean different things. Is it a common set of rules that can be applied to HR, or is it about the management of a group of people who work globally?... Global means that there is a common set of rules that can be applied to all countries'
Chief Information Officer

BOX 1

Challenges facing global HR functions

- The consequences of global business process redesign, the pursuit of a global centre of excellence strategy and the global redistribution and relocation of work that this often entails.
- The absorption of acquired businesses from what might previously have been competitor businesses, attempts to develop and harmonise core HR processes within these merged businesses, and the management of growth through the process of acquisition whereby new country operations are often built around the purchase of a series of national teams.
- The rapid start-up of international operations and the requirement to provide insights into the organisation development needs of new operations as they mature through different stages of the business life cycle.
- The changing capabilities of international operations as many skills become obsolescent very quickly and as changes in the organisational structure and design expose managers to more complex roles that require a general up-skilling of local operations.
- Capitalising on technology and ensuring that local social and cultural insights are duly considered when it is imperative to do so and especially when IT is being used to centralise and 'transactionalise' HR processes, or to create shared services, on a global basis.
- Understanding the changes being wrought in the HR service supply chain as the need for several intermediary service providers is being reduced, and as web-based HR provision is leading to greater individualisation of HRM across international operations that often currently have very different levels of 'HR sophistication'.
- Determining the levels of performance that can be delivered to the business, and the requirement to meet these pledges often under conditions of cost control across international operations, or shareholder pressure for the delivery of rapid financial returns in new international operations.
- Learning how to operate through formal or informal global HR networks, how to act as knowledge brokers across international operations, and how not to pursue automatically a one-best-way HR philosophy.
- Offering a compelling value proposition to the employees of the organisation, understanding and then marketing the brand that the organisation represents across global labour markets that have different values and different perceptions.
- Managing the identity issues faced by HR professionals as they experience changes in the level of decentralisation/centralisation across constituent international businesses. As knowledge and ideas about best practice flow from both the centre to the operations and vice versa, it is not uncommon for HR professionals at all levels of the organisation to feel that their ideas are being overridden by those of other nationalities or business systems.

This chapter reviews:

- **The key competencies for successful global HR**
- **The importance of international transactions, capability development and business development**
- **The qualities of a good global HR professional**

3 | Keys to success for global HR

So how do you ensure your global HR function is successful? Our survey provided a very clear view of the key competencies required from the HR function in an international organisation (see Figure 4).

In line with our comments on the difference between domestic and international HR in Chapter 2, it is interesting to note that the two competencies seen to be most critical were, first, acting as a strategic partner, closely followed by the need to ensure flexibility in all HR programmes and processes. While this all sounds good in theory, we need to look at what our global HR professionals 'actually do' in order to see if they can deliver the needs of organisations in a more globalised world.

Global HR activities

From our members' survey we were able to identify three separate dimensions to their global HRM activities (see Figure 5 overleaf):

- international transactions
- capability development
- business development.

Figure 4 | Competencies for the global HR function

The most internationalised activities were communication processes, recruitment and selection, pay and benefits, training and development and performance management. The least internationalised activities concerned employment law, equality and diversity, cost-reduction initiatives, process re-engineering and industrial relations.

It is easy to assume that the transactional work will be automated and that this presents a major threat to the careers of HR professionals. But the situation is neither as simple nor as stark as this. The proportion of HR professionals in the international transactions, capability development and business development roles were 33 per cent, 31 per cent and 36 per cent respectively. This would suggest that around one-third of the HR professionals are 'at risk' from wide-scale use of e-enabled HR, but two-thirds are already skilled in the two most important areas.

Moving to a strategic role: capability development

One of the most vital roles for global HR functions is the need to build and develop the capabilities of the organisation. Many organisations have been using the opportunities afforded by new technology to create the 'space' for new 'capability development' roles among their global HR professionals. These roles are focused on the most significant business issues, and the need to build and develop capabilities within the organisation, rather than constantly reacting to the traditional performance management, transactional and international assignment issues.

The international capability agenda is more concerned with the up-skilling of a business function, and with spending more time engaging with the leadership teams of these functions than the traditional developmental activities. Attending

Figure 5 | Three dimensions to the global HR professional role

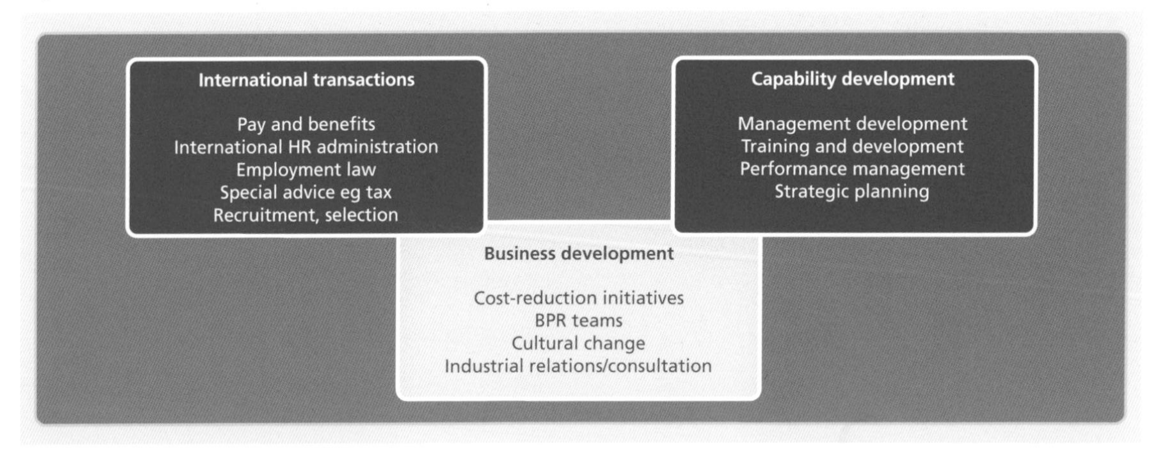

to these fundamental issues of business capability has been made easier by the removal of some layers of management.

With global lines of business there is a more immediate relationship between the global HR professional and the global leadership teams within major business functions or markets. The role of the global HR professional shifts towards being able to answer the sorts of question shown in Box 2 within each of these global functions.

BOX 2
Key questions about the organisational capability

- What state is the function in?
- Where is our 'talent pipeline'?
- What are the key roles within the business in which we really need to have our top people?
- Who are our top people?
- How do you develop them to get to those key positions?
- How do we build succession cover for those key positions?
- What level of understanding is there about the links between the business agenda and the capabilities of the people, and what is the potential for mobility around these people?
- What does a calibration of talent on a global basis suggest for business development?

Talent management and employer branding

A critical part of developing organisational capability is the ability to recruit, retain and develop outstanding talent around the world. Issues of employer branding and talent management are intimately linked for most global organisations. This involves constantly reselling the proposition to employees of why their organisation is the place they should work. The challenge is to understand what makes a really good person want to stay with the company *globally*.

These messages cannot be aspirational – they have to be grounded in what the organisation really offers and what potential employees really want. The processes must back up what the organisation says it is. The key messages to potential employees also must make sense in all the organisation's markets worldwide. The organisation has to pick out which messages they can match and where they are able to give out a message that can be fulfilled. Each market has cultural differences but also similarities.

'...The company is global and will be able to offer some things the same across all markets. We need to focus on similarities and not get bogged down in differences... We won't come up with things that mean the same in all parts of the world, as it's impossible, but we can come up with something unique to us that resonates with people throughout the businesses.'
Global Resourcing Director

The challenge for global organisations is to decide what the overriding message is of who they are and what they stand for. This thinking about talent on a global basis is leading organisations towards a series of common responses:

- Researching into 'consumer insights' with current and potential employees, sister companies and external agencies, and benchmarking with external companies.
- Managing the 'talent pipeline' – trying to recruit 'ahead of the curve' instead of the more traditional vacancy-based recruitment.
- Communicating an awareness in graduate schools and businesses to get the people they are looking for.
- Developing internal talent pools around the world.
- Creating skilled and competent teams of assessors in different regional geographies.
- Managing recruitment suppliers on a global basis, introducing speed, cost and quality controls, establishing master contracts to co-ordinate the messages conveyed and the use of preferred partners, ensuring audit trails to protect against legal issues associated with global diversity.
- E-enabling jobs notice boards, redesigning websites to convey important messages about the employer brand.

This type of approach is particularly important for an organisation like Diageo, with a global brand name. To raise the recruiting excellence of the company, it has to recruit from a global perspective, rather than take on local people who then have to travel all over the world. Such a company needs to search for talent in countries outside those where it has existing operations. For example, for its US operation Diageo recently recruited in India and South Korea.

Diageo has set up a global network project around recruitment and talent development, to be led by the HR community in the USA, given its knowledge about the recruitment issues. This network does not look at issues in the old HR way – considering whether the ideas are technically great. Its very existence – and the endorsement of any projects undertaken – depends on the ability of the HR leader to write a strategy paper that stands up against a brands strategy or other business strategies. The network then has the endorsement to look at key issues globally, not just locally, considers the HR learning from initiatives such as setting up a global brand team, and then reviews how HR can add value. Evaluation is based not just on success of implementation but also on embedding ideas within the businesses. Work has been carried out to examine the 'employer brand' – finding out the message that is sent to potential consumers (ie employees), whether the type of people being recruited have brand awareness and can quote what the brand benefit statement is. Diageo examined its reputation in its major markets such as the USA, UK, Ireland and Spain.

Creating a career site and an employer brand was considered to be critical to the messages being given to consumers.

How does the function deliver organisational capability?

In order to deliver organisational capability, global HR functions need appropriate delivery mechanisms, such as e-enabled systems and global centres of excellence, as we discussed in Chapter 1. In addition, we found that in the light of HR affordability considerations, the use of global HR networks was becoming a critical success factor in this area.

Working through global HR networks

Networking has always been important within global HR. Historically, global information, insight into local conditions and best practice have all tended to be shared through the process of global HR professionals just talking to each other – getting groups of people together within the organisation to facilitate the transfer of learning. The intention now is to formalise the process, so that they can work within existing networks. Networks also suit a model of global HR that is oriented towards more decentralisation and centres of excellence.

Within Diageo, for example, half a dozen global HR networks were established around strategically important initiatives such as recruitment and employer branding, performance and reward, organisation development, and international assignments. These global networks are not just put in place for the purpose of knowledge transfer. They are used increasingly to cut through bureaucracy and to act as important decision-making groups (see Box 3).

'...If you're in HR in a global company and you want to make something happen, you need to get people together from across the businesses. So we use global networks both to get big business ideas to come to life and to give an opportunity to talented people in HR and elsewhere to get a global perspective and work on a major international project.'
Global Resourcing Director

BOX 3
The role of informal global networks

- Provide a forum to encourage innovation and growth throughout the business and a vehicle to get the right people onto the right teams in order to make this happen.
- Encourage HR professionals and line managers to think beyond their 'own patch'.
- Create a 'win/win scenario' whereby membership of the network provides advantages to both the line managers and the HR professionals.
- Get stakeholders (the senior HR community, business leaders) to buy into the business change.
- Force the business agenda in subtle ways.

One of our case studies, Shell People Services (SPS), has been experimenting with global expertise networks that also serve a knowledge management role. The rationale of SPS is to provide common HR services to group companies and to participate in setting the group's HR direction and policies. A critical success factor in being able to meet these goals is to maintain a repository of HR knowledge and expertise. Shell has developed several successful global communities, which enable practitioners in a particular field to 'meet' other practitioners and exchange ideas, problems and best practice. Global HR staff are located over three continents and increasingly need to share information and work in virtual teams. So that all HR staff, regardless of geographical location, can access and use an information store of best practice, SPS has pursued a strategy based on selecting pilot global HR teams with a proven need for collaborative working and team sharing. The lessons that emerge from the operation of these networks are shown in Box 4 opposite.

What does this mean for the global HR professional?

We believe that the new roles for international HR professionals highlight the need for them to develop important personal competencies related to key process skills, political skills and technical knowledge. The attributes most frequently evident in the work of the professionals we studied were:

- being a strategic thinker
- possession of strong personal networks inside and outside the organisation
- being a provider of information and advice within this business network
- becoming a broker of appropriate knowledge, learning and ideas across a loose connection of people
- capacity for and tolerance of the ambiguities and uncertainties inherent in new business situations
- being a resource negotiator
- being a process facilitator, with diplomatic sensitivity to complex organisational politics and power struggles
- mobilising the energy and engagement behind ideas
- having a respect for the countries and communities being dealt with
- showing an appreciation of the ways in which culture influences core organisational behaviours
- the capacity to work virtually.

To do this, professionals need to be able to understand, develop an insight into and take an overview of the links between HR processes and effective business performance across the global network.

BOX 4

Lessons from the management of formal global expertise networks

- In order to build on the 'social capital' that resides within these communities, HR professionals have to build relationships. Strong relationships still require considerable face-to-face contact.
- The communities have to work on real business issues.
- The technology enables, but does not cause, the required connections and sharing.
- One size does not fit all – each HR process is at a different stage of evolution.
- Global HR networks vary, based on the size of the HR community, the character of the HR disciplines comprising the network, customer needs, relative levels of regional versus global focus, and the relationships that the global network leader has with one or more core HR processes.

This chapter examines three main types of evaluation for global HRM:

- **High-impact projects**
- **Service-level agreements**
- **Performance pledges**

4 | Evaluating the contribution of the global HRM role

The way in which the global HR function is evaluated clearly depends on which aspect of its activity is under scrutiny. However, our study revealed three main types of evaluation.

- **Evaluating high-impact projects**
  Where the global HR function is involved in the delivery of a major business transformation project, as above, then the evaluation is very much based on a psychological contract set between the Chief Executive and the senior global HR manager. Promises and expectations are mutually established as the function embarks on a major organisation development initiative.

- **Service-level agreements (SLAs)**
  Where global HR is operating as a shared service provider to the organisation as a whole, it tends to be operating under a commercial model. For the more transactional areas of activity, then, the evaluation is contractual, and is often supported by SLA arrangements.

- **Performance pledges**
  For the global HR function as a whole, the evaluation, where it exists, tends to be based on performance promises to the business, often in the format of a balanced scorecard arrangement, with associated key performance indicators.

We outline some of the developments taking place, but the following quotation seems to capture the current situation:

> ***'...Accountants took 100 years to work out how to measure the value that financial resources have – the language that you use and so on. They now have understanding and as such it is a language of business. HR should now be aspiring to something similar – but we are a long way from that yet.'***
> **Global HR Expert Service Provider**

Evaluating high-impact projects

Former Prime Minister Harold Macmillan, when asked what he feared most in politics, reputedly answered: 'Events, dear boy, events!' In the world of global HR too, events can change the situation overnight. For example, the September 11 attack on the USA, coupled with a slowing down of global growth, had a significant impact on a number of our case-study organisations. Most of the functions we analysed were working on significant change initiatives set against very tight deadlines. As one instance, BOC Group embarked on a major change process to put all its North and

South Asian operations into a global line of business (LOB) structure from a previous regional structure. BOC initiated a move towards a new business structure based on a global LOB model over three years ago. The work necessary to align HR operations with the new global structure was scheduled to take place over two years. The successful implementation of changes elsewhere in the business, however, meant that the global HR function must redesign structures and operations within a one-year, not a two-year, timetable.

Global HR professionals are often now engaged in similar projects, which require them to help the organisation design the structural, role and capability requirements that follow the adoption of global lines of business. Several of our case studies had significant organisation development and internal consulting groups operating under the umbrella of their global HR function. Not surprisingly, then, the function tends to evaluate itself against a range of 'project success' metrics. Box 5 shows the critical success factors established at BOC by which global HR intervention would be judged.

BOX 5
Critical success factors for development implementation in a global HR organisation

- Consistency with a global HR model where possible.
- Compliance with global HR systems and processes.
- Cost-effectiveness, with HR delivery against comparative benchmarks.
- Ability to deliver 'best practice' HR functionality.
- Ability to share learning across business units.
- Long-term efficiency through the use of HR systems and e-enablement.
- Sensitivity to statutory and cultural requirements within geographies.
- Developing a balance between local talent and home country resources/attraction of new regional HR talent.

Engineering service-level agreements (SLAs)

Given the increasing use of benchmarking, market-testing and outsourcing, SLAs are being used as a form of contract between departments. It is clear that when an internal client asks the global HR function 'Have you got any benchmarking data?' what the client really means is 'Show us that you are not expensive.' Global HR functions are trying to turn this conversation into one where they can say 'Yes, we have that data, but we think that benchmarking is limited for your real needs.'

In Shell, for example, SLAs are used to evaluate a number of services to the global businesses (see Box 6 opposite).

BOX 6
Areas of evaluation for international HR in an SLA

- Customer satisfaction forms used to evaluate performance in terms of responsiveness, quality of delivery, value for money, professional expertise and speed of billing.
- Costs are specified for consulting support across a range of activities on a per day basis.
- Expatriation: with payroll services, tax advice, work permits, residence permits, spouse employment consultancy, temporary assignees specified on a per case or per month of administration basis.
- Outplacement staff support and workshops advised on a per client basis.
- Learning: consulting, event organisation and administration and event delivery.
- Talent pipeline: selection fees per recruit for graduates, MBAs, experienced managers; licensing fees for best-practice tools and techniques; executive search; project management.
- HR data and application services; diversity; compensation and job evaluation; organisation development and change management.

Clearly, establishing SLAs is a time-consuming process, hence it is important to be clear as to their purpose (see Box 7).

BOX 7
The key purposes of SLAs as a form of evaluation in global HR

- Define the product and services to be provided
- Establish the manner in which the products and services will be delivered
- Establish quality standards to be achieved
- Establish measurement criteria
- Establish reporting criteria
- Negotiate and determine the cost of delivery

The advantages of using SLAs are that they:

- articulate the connection between the global HR function's vision, mission and strategic targets, and the way in which it actually operates
- establish a two-way accountability for service and impose a service management discipline on both parties
- encourage the service provider to examine its service provision, bringing a sense of clarity to the relationships, support levels and commitments
- build on the thought process behind total quality management and business process re-engineering by establishing critical levels of service and standardised expectations

- remove levels of unpredictability and help foster more accurate levels of resource prediction

- define clear criteria for service evaluation.

Increasingly, global HR functions are using SLAs to provide a 'high-level' description of their overall service – with some measures of how they can test whether the service is on track and what levels of demand customers are forecasting.

Performance pledges

An alternative to the use of SLAs is the adoption of high-level performance pledges. This was seen, for example, in Diageo, and a similar system based on a balanced scorecard approach was used within Ford of Europe.

In Diageo the performance of all businesses is measured against the business strategy, using an instrument called a 'performance promise'. These promises are brief – they can be written on one page – but they create an implicit link between the business strategy and the focus of activity in the function and a metric for establishing whether the function has delivered against these linkages. The performance propositions are based around the linking activities. They identify the key result areas required from each business and the evidence of these particular actions. The promises therefore 'bind' a senior leadership team into the strategy. They are backed up by an entrepreneurial reward system and are negotiated with the Diageo Executive Committee. HR is tied into a performance promise along with every other business function.

We began this chapter by pointing to the importance of global HR functions being able to deliver against quite personalised business relationships. The performance pledge – and the negotiation of any balanced scorecard – is in essence a series of implicit business contracts formed between each function (business partner) and the business as a whole. Delivering against these promises becomes the major way through which the global HR function and its leaders will establish long-term credibility.

This chapter outlines:

- **The delivery mechanisms for global HRM**
- **A framework for diagnosing a company's global HR positioning**

5 | What diagnostic frameworks and processes help the global HR function be an effective contributor?

A new model of global HRM

Our study provides a unique opportunity to grasp the nature of global HRM. We present in Figure 6 a model illustrating the essence of this approach to coherence and consistency in global HRM.

Figure 6 | Delivery mechanisms

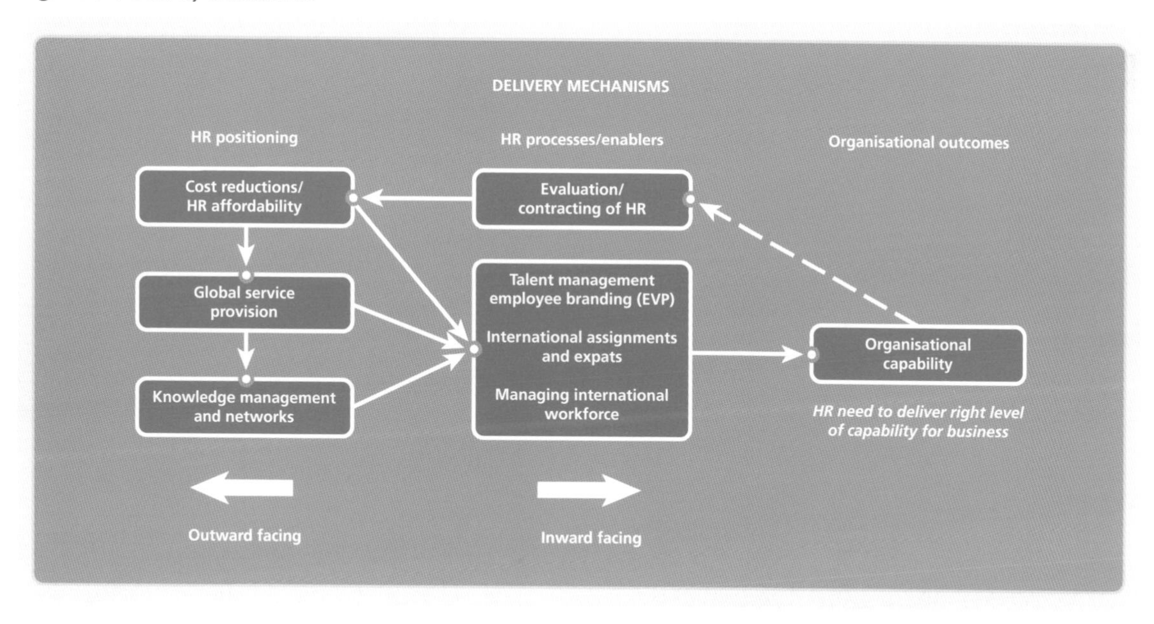

The model identifies the key mechanisms by which global HRM delivers organisational capability; it also summarises the discussion so far. As we have seen earlier in this Briefing, leading-edge global HR functions are acutely aware of the need to 'position' themselves so as to deliver the processes that will lead to organisational capability. This involves the following:

HR positioning

1 **Cost reductions/HR affordability:** as indicated, a key driving force behind recent restructuring efforts of most global HR functions has been the need to deliver global business strategies in the most cost-efficient manner possible. This reinforces the distinctions between activities of a purely *transactional* nature and those that are concerned with *capability* and *business development*.

2 **Global service provision:** a combination of centres of excellence and e-HR as the key delivery mechanisms for global HR. This has clear implications in terms of the level of expertise sought at selection and the amount of training given by the organisation, including access to CIPD qualifications.

3 **Knowledge management and networks:** perhaps the most critical component in terms of HR positioning lies in its role as knowledge management champion operating through the development of networks.

HR processes

Effective positioning creates a global HR function that is able to deliver value in the three key processes we have identified as constituting global HRM, namely:

- talent management/employer branding
- international assignment management
- managing a global workforce.

This three-way split emphasises a move away from the traditional perspective of international HRM, which was concerned mainly with the management of global assignments.

Talent management on a global basis is a far broader concept than plotting a series of international assignments for young high-potentials. In order to attract and retain the best talent anywhere in the world, an organisation must have a strong and positive employer brand. A key challenge for international organisations is the extent to which it is possible to create global employee value propositions (EVPs).

International assignment management remains a critical component of effective global HR, particularly in relation to the use of international assignments as mechanisms for developing global leaders. Once again, we see the need for a far more strategic perspective to the management of international assignments. Organisations are actively considering ways of measuring the value of international assignments and are investigating alternatives to international working in the form of long-term assignments. A key question global HR professionals and line managers should be asking is: why are expatriates from head office mostly used when the organisation is espousing a geocentric or global orientation?

Managing a global workforce reflects changes in the role of global HR. Our study has revealed an increasing emphasis on globalising HR processes, with intense discussion around what needs to be global versus regional versus national. This new definition of global HR positions the global HR professional as the guardian of culture, operating global values and systems.

Organisational capability

All our actions under HR positioning and HR processes, as discussed above, need to be directed towards the ultimate outcome of the model, namely, delivering organisational capability. In order to achieve this, the global HR director and his or her team must work with the senior management team at a global level to create and implement global organisational strategy. Our study provides evidence of this strategic role for HR, with nearly two-thirds of respondents to our survey either being on the main board of directors or reporting directly to the main board.

Diagnosing your global HR positioning

The results of our study allow you to reflect on your current level of globalisation within your HR function through the following diagnostic frameworks:

- stage reached on model of global HRM
- positioning on the three main roles of global HR professionals
- evaluation of effectiveness of your global HR function.

1 Stage reached on model of global HRM

How is your global HR function configured in order to maximise cost reductions and to provide the most efficient service delivery? To what extent are you seen to be a knowledge management champion, not only for your own function, but also as a support for broader organisational knowledge-sharing?

2 Positioning on the three main roles of global HR professionals

It is useful to analyse the percentage of HR resources that are currently allocated to each of the three main roles and to consider whether this is the best model to deliver organisational capability in the most cost-effective manner.

3 Evaluation of effectiveness of your global HR function

Probably the most effective way of assessing where you stand in terms of becoming a truly global HR function is to ask your internal and external clients. Using a 360-degree approach, we recommend you plot your function against the following criteria:

- **Strategic business partner:** eg is the corporate HR function always a part of the organisation's strategic planning team?
- **Networks:** eg to what extent has your corporate HR function developed networks with line managers in all countries in which your organisation operates?
- **Competencies of global HR professionals:** eg what language skills do your global HR professionals possess?
- **Cost benefit:** eg to what extent does your corporate HR function positively contribute to the bottom line of your organisation?
- **Organisational relevance:** eg to what extent do you think that your corporate HR function plays a critical role in the development of the organisation's values, mission and business planning?

Effectiveness can also be assessed through the same 360-degree feedback technique by asking clients to assess the performance of the HR function in all its major activities along various dimensions, such as:

- effectiveness of service delivery
- insight into local market conditions.

Using these three diagnostic techniques will allow you to evaluate the reality of your current level of globalisation and identify the critical areas you need to address to move to your desired state.

Conclusion

Organisations are internationalising their HRM as they endeavour to survive against global competition. Our study has identified both the strategic pressures facing global HR functions and their responses. These activities are heralding a significant shift in the nature of HR away from the traditional concerns of international HRM functions (managing an internationally mobile workforce) towards the concerns of a global HR function (the need to manage international HRM activities through the application of a global set of rules to HRM processes). There is a much stronger focus on cross-country and cross-function business issues.

The implication of these changes for HR professionals is quite profound. In particular, HR professionals have to ensure that the activities they engage in move them away from more transactional types of work towards those concerned with developing organisational capability and business development. HR professionals have to develop the expertise and the competencies necessary for working through global networks. These networks are serving two purposes: helping to transfer knowledge and cultural insight across global operations; and acting as a decision-making forum that brings the right people together to make things happen in the organisation. As they engage in these activities, global HR managers are becoming the guardians of national culture – helping to define where the new line in the sand is drawn between globally standardised and localised HR practices.

Clearly, the more that the HR function can justify its value and contribution to this process of globalisation, the less it needs be concerned with questions about the affordability of the function. Evaluation is a critical task. It is being achieved in three main ways: through the adoption of change project metrics that not only measure successful execution of strategy but also the extent to which the changes are engaged with by line managers; through the use of tightly specified service-level agreements to measure issues of speed, cost and quality; and through the creation of high-level performance promises (performance management contracts) from the HR function to the other global functions.

In practice, most organisations are gradually making this transition from international to global HR. The research has helped to identify the questions that need to be asked to help guide organisations down this path, and the ways in which they can measure the effectiveness of their global HR function. This is in terms of its being a strategic business partner; its having developed the networks and relationships with business managers; and the competencies of its global HR professionals.